THE OFFICIAL
LIVERPOOL FC
ANNUAL 2004

YOU'LL NEVER WALK ALONE

LIVERPOOL
FOOTBALL CLUB

EST·1892 ®

THE OFFICIAL
LIVERPOOL FC
ANNUAL 2004

YOU'LL NEVER WALK ALONE

LIVERPOOL
FOOTBALL CLUB

EST · 1892 ®

G
E
R
A
R
D
H
O
U
L
L
I
E
R

Going for gold

GERARD HOULLIER SAYS LIVERPOOL WILL BUILD UPON THE EXPERIENCES OF LAST SEASON AND BELIEVES HIS SQUAD NEEDS A BIT MORE TIME TO ACHIEVE GREATNESS

There's no doubt about it. The Reds' manager is disappointed not to be taking his players on a tour of the top European arenas this year, but he insists his squad will benefit from suffering the disappointment of only finishing fifth in last season's Premiership.

As he puts it: "We finished fifth last season and we won a final against Manchester United. I wouldn't say it was a disappointing season but we can improve. When you progress like we have in the last four years, you do get phases when some players are not as good as they have been previously. We experienced a phase of plateau but I was expecting that to come at some stage."

Houllier puts the slump in the middle of the season down to a number of factors. Among them was the loss in form of several key players, some of whom had played in the World Cup and badly needed a break. He insists that Liverpool didn't lose the Champions League place at Chelsea on the final day, but let it slip far earlier during the Championship.

"There were a few games when we had chances to finish teams off and didn't, which gave the opposition more confidence. On top of that, our home record was not good enough. Before the Chelsea game, the statistics showed that only Manchester United had more shots than we did, so we do attack – we are not negative – but unfortunately we lacked the clinical finish at times and we were

not as strong or solid at the back as we have been in recent seasons.

"When we did attack, two things went wrong. The finishing wasn't equal to the number of chances we created – Sunderland's Jurgen Macho had two great games all season and they were both against us – and around the box we weren't effective enough. We scored practically as many goals as the season before but conceded 11 more. That was one of our fortes the year before.

"Crucially we missed Didi Hamann for a number of months and Steven Gerrard when he went through his bad patch and costly suspension. Plus we were without Stephane Henchoz for almost half the season. He's a good, strong, experienced defender and we missed him. These problems provide an explanation, not an excuse, and we want to work on them. We know we have under-achieved but I still feel we need a bit more time.

"This squad has been rebuilt in my

time here, we have won six trophies and reached the Champions League twice. That has been excellent. But last season some players prospered and some didn't. We must keep the nucleus and do better."

Houllier denies claims that his side aren't attack-minded enough but he does admit that his defence – so often the rock-solid foundation for success during his Anfield reign so far – weren't as effective last season.

He says: "Elimination from the Champions League affected the morale of the players and – allied to the fact our home form was not as good as it had been – we slipped up.

"If you look at our away form, it was very good. I think things started to go wrong after the game against Basel.

"I don't accept some of the criticism we have had, particularly when people say we are not an attacking team. When you look at the stats and the number of shots on goal we are second only to Manchester United. In total, we had 502 shots, while Arsenal had only 485."

Houllier believes the Reds played plenty of good football but that the defence did not always perform to their usual standards. He also points out that the team played 19 games at home last season and scored in 17 of them.

"I am happy with the team spirit and I believe we will bounce back. The criticism is partly down to the fact that the expectations of our fans have risen sharply because of what we have achieved in four seasons."

Houllier admits he was hurt by some of the criticism which came his way during the last difficult campaign, but that hasn't shaken his desire to take the Reds back to the top of the English game. However, he insists fans should give his players time to close the gap on Manchester United.

"Our vision and our goal is the Premiership," he says. "There's no doubt about that. But at the top level the age difference is a factor and in that respect we need a bit of time.

"Don't get me wrong, we have some experienced players in our squad but the average age of the team at Chelsea on the last day of last season was just 25 compared to Chelsea's average age of 29. That makes a difference.

"This season I want us to get back into the top three. That is the aim. The players can learn from the bad spell we went through last season. It was an average season and we can do better. I'm a great believer that you don't achieve anything in life without going through a bad period and this season has really tested us. Whether it's in your social, private or professional life, there will always come a time when you need to go through a period of adversity. We will be better for what we went through last season.

"I know there was a lot of criticism of me last season but I never had any doubts about myself. I always question myself. Can I put things right? Can I improve things?

"I learned a lot about the way I am viewed at this club during the poor spell and it was good to see the players' and the board's reaction to the speculation about my future. I have no plans to stop. I will go on for as long as I can. If there is no more petrol in the tank I will stop. That is not the case at the moment.

"At some stage you have to go through a difficult period. No pain without gain. That has fired me up even more for this season. I've never felt as good as I am now. I will stay a manager as long as I can – I have no deadlines on that." ⊕

MICHAEL'S MAGIC TOUCH

> While the country continues to be engulfed in 'Rooney-Mania', it would be easy to forget that the original Boy Wonder is still one of the shining lights of English football.

If anyone is well-placed to advise Everton star Rooney on the constant scrutiny and analysis which lies in wait for him as he continues his footballing development, it's Liverpool star Michael Owen.

Owen has been treading the path Rooney is currently embarking on ever since he scored that goal against Argentina in the 1998 World Cup finals.

It was a career-defining strike from the young England star – and he hasn't looked back since as he has gone on to establish himself as one of the best goalscorers on the European and world stages.

But it hasn't all been plain sailing for Gerard Houllier's coveted striking star. True, he now has worldwide fame and a lifestyle that the vast majority of kids could only ever dream of, but with that fame come the pitfalls and there have been plenty of them during an astonishing first five years in professional football for Owen.

It's almost a newspaper headline whenever he fails to score a goal – and it's certainly deemed a crisis if he dares to let a series of games slip by without hitting the net. The English press are renowned for building

up players to superstar status only to knock them down again at the first opportunity. Owen must have a hundred tales to tell by now of incidents and events which have led to him being unfairly criticised in the media.

But, to his credit, he has remained mentally strong and has come through each of his bad spells in the best way he knows – with an avalanche of goals.

By his own admission, injuries were casting a huge shadow over his career a couple of years ago. The curse of the hamstring was striking at regular intervals, while in his mind he must have always been wondering when the next setback was going to come along.

"I'm working hard every day before training to stick to a fitness programme the medical staff have devised for me and, touch wood, it seems to be working because I haven't missed too many games over recent months," says Owen.

"I knew I was going to have to do something because the injuries were getting me down. I went through some bad times when I never knew from one game to the next if my hamstring was going to go again. But I'm happy in my own mind that the problems are over now and I can look forward to the future with confidence."

Liverpool can certainly look to the future with confidence while they continue to have Owen in their ranks. Having had a rare summer off this year with no international competition to play in, club boss Gerard Houllier is expecting big things from his number one striker.

Houllier says: "It's been a long time since Michael has had an extended rest from football and been able to go away and just relax.

"I have always said that a striker's

> **BEING AT LIVERPOOL MEANS THAT YOU WILL PLAY IN A LOT OF HIGH-PROFILE GAMES AND THE RECORDS TELL YOU THAT MICHAEL SCORES IN THE BIG GAMES. HE IS A BIG-GAME PLAYER**

best years come when they get to 27 or 28 so Michael is still a while away from being at his peak. But, having said that, I think he will be awesome for us this season.

"His all-round game is improving all the time and some of his performances for us of late have been phenomenal. Of course, he will always score goals but his work rate is first-class and his movement is excellent. He is getting better and better and I am pleased he is now getting the rewards for all the work he is putting in to protect him from injury problems.

"Being at Liverpool means that you will play in a lot of high-profile games and the records tell you that Michael performs, i.e. scores, in the big games. He is a big-game player and I really like that about him."

Houllier's admiration for Owen is also shared by many of his team-mates.

Norwegian full-back John Arne Riise says, "Michael is one of the best players in the world.

"I knew about him before I came here but he continues to amaze me. With everything he has already achieved in the game, you'd think he'd been around for ever and it's incredible to think he's only been in the first team for five years. He's a great player and he's going to score lots and lots more goals for Liverpool."

Those sentiments are echoed by German midfielder Dietmar Hamann, who adds, "People always make out there's some kind of crisis when Michael doesn't score a goal but that just goes to show how good a player he is. Expectations of him are so high.

"Even when he goes a few games without scoring we always know it will just be a matter of time before he's banging them in again. He has proved himself so many times now for club and country. We are lucky to have a player of his ability here and people shouldn't forget that."

So, while Wayne Rooney may be the new kid on the Merseyside block you'd still be hard-pressed to find a Liverpool fan – or maybe even a fan of any club – who would swap Owen for the Everton star. ⊕

MICHAEL'S STATS FOR CLUB AND COUNTRY UP TO MAY 2003

1ST TEAM GAMES	258
1ST TEAM GOALS	140
ENGLAND CAPS	47
ENGLAND GOALS	20

JERZY DUDEK

DOB 23 MARCH 1973 **NATIONALITY** POLISH **POSITION** GOALKEEPER **NICKNAME** THE DUDE
HEIGHT 6' 1 **WEIGHT** 12st 7lbs **SQUAD NUMBER** 1 **PREVIOUS CLUBS** SOKOL TYCHY, FEYENOORD

1 When Jerzy was growing up, what did his father do for a living?

2 How many other Polish players have ever played for Liverpool?

3 Prior to his move to Anfield, which other Premiership club was he close to joining?

4 Which honour did he win in Holland at the end of the 1998–99 season?

5 Against which country did he make his international debut for Poland?

6 Against which club did he make his Liverpool debut?

7 What was the score in that game?

8 How many clean sheets did he keep for Liverpool in his first 50 games for the club?

9 How many seasons did he play in Holland for Feyenoord?

10 Who said of Dudek when he was with Feyenoord: "He is the best goalkeeper I have seen in 30 years"?

All answers on page 63

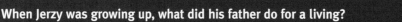

LIVERPOOL'S GOALKEEPING COACH IS FORMER ENGLAND NUMBER ONE JOE CORRIGAN + + + EMILE HESKEY DONATED A

1. Against which team did Kirkland make his Coventry debut?
2. Where was Kirkland born?
3. In what year did he make his first appearance in the Premiership?
4. What was the score when Kirkland played at Anfield for Coventry in November 2000?
5. In which competition did he make his first appearance for Liverpool?
6. Against which team did that debut take place?
7. Which other player was involved in the incident which saw him damage his cruciate knee ligaments in January 2003?
8. What was the name of the doctor who assessed his injury in America?
9. How many Merseyside derbies has Chris played in so far?
10. Which team did he support as a boy?

DOB 2 MAY 1981 **NATIONALITY** ENGLISH **POSITION** GOALKEEPER **NICKNAME** KIRKY
HEIGHT 6'6 **WEIGHT** 14st 4lbs **SQUAD NUMBER** 22 **PREVIOUS CLUBS** COVENTRY

CHRIS KIRKLAND

88 MINS

The 2002-03 season may not be remembered as one of the best in Liverpool's illustrious history, but it contained a date and a match which will be remembered by Reds' fans all over the world for a long, long time.

March 2 was the date, Cardiff's Millennium Stadium was the venue and arch-rivals Manchester United were the opponents in the Worthington Cup final. Whether you were in the stadium or watching at home on a TV screen, you'll never forget the moment when Steven Gerrard scored another of his crackers and Michael Owen blasted home from close range to kill off United's challenge and give Gerard Houllier's men a memorable win against their rivals from down the M62.

United were everyone's favourites to win. Liverpool had only recently emerged from a league slump whereas Alex Ferguson's men were setting off on the kind of run which would ultimately lead them to title glory.

But Liverpool had revenge on their minds following their league defeat at Anfield to United in December and, right from the first whistle in Cardiff, it was clear one team wanted it more than the other.

Gerrard and Owen got the goals but the Reds were also indebted to Man of the Match Jerzy Dudek who pulled off a series of super saves to keep United out.

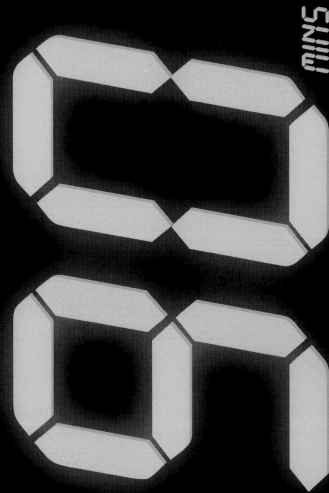

THE FOLLOWING TOOK PLACE BETWEEN 3.00PM AND 4.45PM ON MARCH 2ND 2003…

1 Liverpool get the game under way, wearing all-red

1 Long Riise pass too strong for Owen and Barthez gathers

3 Murphy strike floors Neville who needs treatment

7 Barthez catches the ball under pressure from Heskey

9 United build on the edge of the box but Van Nistelrooy's pass is too strong

12 Hamann slides the ball towards Heskey but Barthez is out quickly to clear the danger

39 MINS

45 Owen sprints at goal but Ferdinand does just enough to put him off

47 Heskey goes down in the box but no penalty given

50 Long ball played through to Owen but he can't reach it

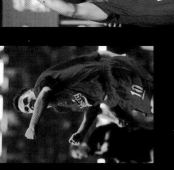

86 MINS

Worthington Cup
WINNERS 2003

Worthington Cup
THE FINAL

Worthington Cup
WINNERS
2003

Worthington Cup
THE FINAL

G **12** Booking: Stephane Henchoz: Foul on Scholes

13 Right-footed shot from Giggs well held by Dudek

T **15** Barthez clears again as Gerrard sends Heskey through on goal

17 Diouf's cross drifts over the goal after good Liverpool possession

21 Giggs cross to Van Nistelrooy who turns his first-time shot inches wide of the far post. Best chance so far

O **29** Riise cuts in from the left and fires tamely at Barthez. Our first shot of the game so far

34 Great run by Owen and a low shot which is well saved

N **36** Murphy curls an effort from the edge of the area over the bar

39 GOAL! Steven Gerrard: Right-footed shot deflected off Beckham over Barthez into the top corner

42 Heskey whips in great cross from the right but United clear

C **43** Henchoz with an amazing clearance on the line to deny Scholes

45 Beckham free-kick straight at Dudek

U **45** Great wing play by Diouf and a good cross which United clear for a corner

48 United get the second half under way attacking towards their own fans

P

52 Murphy's first-time shot is caught by Barthez

54 Great defending by Hamann stops Reds conceding a corner

59 Dudek makes a great save from van Nistelrooy

60 Diouf shoots low but Barthez has no problems

63 Amazing run by Baros and then great shot from Gerrard saved well

63 Hyypia heads straight at Barthez from a corner

65 Great save from Dudek after a good effort from Scholes

69 Murphy's close range shot hits Baros in the United area

70 Beckham miskicks in front of Dudek's goal

71 Van Nistelrooy wastes a clear chance to score when Dudek saves his shot well

72 Diouf goes on a run but he fails to shoot on goal

81 Brilliant save from Dudek denies van Nistelrooy as United pile on the pressure

86 GOAL! Michael Owen: Great low strike past Barthez after Hamann pass

87 United fans streaming out of the ground!

89 Smicer almost scores after great play from Murphy

90 The ref blows his whistle and it's all over. Liverpool have beaten their arch rivals 2-0. The fans and players go wild

BEHIND THE SCENES

LIVERPOOL FC
– BEHIND THE SCENES

IF YOU THINK LIFE AT LIVERPOOL FC IS ALL ABOUT THE MANAGEMENT STAFF AND THEIR SQUAD OF PLAYERS – THEN THINK AGAIN.

It's true that the vast majority of fans, quite rightly, are only interested in what happens on the pitch on a Saturday afternoon – but it's equally true that without the work of many people throughout the week at both Anfield and Melwood then the football wouldn't even take place.

We can't possibly introduce you to every Liverpool FC employee on these pages, but we thought you may be interested to hear a little bit more about the team behind the team at your favourite club.

Let's start off at the stadium – and one of the most important people on a matchday has to be Stadium Manager and Safety Certificate Holder, **Ged Poynton**. Ged works closely with the police and the stewards both in the build-up to games and in the aftermath of games to ensure strict safety guidelines are being followed and that everyone entering the stadium is doing so safely.

"We never compromise on safety," says Ged. "We can't afford to. My job is to make sure that everyone is watching the match in as comfortable and as safe an environment as possible. We work with all the local authorities to make sure this stadium is a safe place to be

and my matchday is never complete until the final supporter has left the stadium and done so safely."

Before a ball has even been kicked on the field the Anfield groundstaff – just like their counterparts at Melwood – will have been working through the week to prepare the surface in exactly the way Gerard Houllier will have requested.

Corporate hospitality is big business in football nowadays and the Reds cater for hundreds of fans every matchday in the 30 executive boxes in the Centenary Stand and the various lounges and suites throughout the stadium. If you want to enjoy the very best matchday hospitality, then make sure you enjoy the full Anfield experience at some stage this season if you possibly can.

All of the club's administrative and

clerical staff are based at Anfield along with chief executive **Rick Parry**, who makes the decisions which will shape the future of the club from his office in the Kop.

Also based at Anfield are the club's PR department along with the 15 full-time staff who work to bring you **Liverpoolfc.tv** – the most visited football website in the world.

Gerard Houllier, as you would expect, is based at Melwood with the rest of his staff. The manager usually arrives at the training ground before 8.30 am and rarely leaves before late afternoon. "We have a wonderful facility here at Melwood and it's very important that our players are given the chance to enjoy their work in the best possible environment," says the boss. "A lot of

work and planning went into the design and building of the complex and we're all very happy with it."

Houllier enjoys his own office at Melwood, as does his assistant **Phil Thompson** while the rest of the coaching staff share a spacious office. The manager isn't too far away from his press officer, whom he deals with regularly during the day, or his secretaries who make his appointments, book his flights and deal with his mail.

With so many foreign players at the club it would be foolish to overlook the fact that many players don't fully understand the English culture – and Liverpool have made sure they don't fall into that trap by employing a full-time Player Liaison officer.

Norman Gard's job is to look after

the foreign players at Liverpool, from organising English lessons to helping them find property or assisting them with their insurance and tax forms. Whatever the player needs, Norman is there to help, advise and assist.

Melwood also houses its own canteen where the players enjoy a morning snack and then a healthy lunch once training is finished and it also provides offices for its medical staff where the club doctor **Mark Waller** and the physiotherapy team carry out their daily duties.

Liverpool FC may exist to win football matches and to win trophies, but never forget that behind the 11 players who wear the red shirt on a Saturday afternoon is another team of hundreds who all play their own small part in making it possible. ⊕

2002

THE 20 DEFINING MOMENTS

AUGUST 11 2002

Liverpool return to the Millennium Stadium, Cardiff, to compete for the Community Shield against Arsenal, but for once lose in South Wales following Gilberto's second half strike. "After this match I saw it as an opportunity to develop the team more and give them more of an attacking licence," commented manager Gerard Houllier.

AUGUST 18 2002

Liverpool open their Premiership campaign with an away clash at Aston Villa and return from the Midlands having collected all three points thanks to John Arne Riise's goal. Danny Murphy creates the opening with a brilliant run through midfield before sliding the ball to Riise who makes no mistake with a low finish into the corner of the goal.

SEPTEMBER 17 2002

A real eye-opener for the Reds as they come unstuck against Valencia in their first Champions League encounter of the season. First-half goals from Pablo Aimar and Ruben Baraja give the Spanish giants a deserved 2–0 win and leave Liverpool in no doubts as to the standard they need to reach to progress in the competition.

SEPTEMBER 25 2002

Liverpool drop more Champions League points following a disappointing 1–1 home draw with little-known Swiss club FC Basel. Despite taking an early lead, the Reds fail to capitalise on the numerous chances they create and pay the penalty when Christian Gross' men equalise before half-time. "We had 29 shots on goal and I can't believe we haven't won," says boss Gerard Houllier.

SEPTEMBER 28 2002

Despite a patchy start to their European adventures for the season, Liverpool are flying in the Premiership and a 3–0 win at Manchester City keeps them right in the hunt at the top of the table. Michael Owen once again sets about silencing his critics with a brilliant hat-trick – his first goals from open play of the campaign.

2003

OCTOBER 6 2002

Michael Owen is again the hero as Liverpool, for the second season running, beat Chelsea at Anfield thanks to a last-minute winner. Owen is on hand in the 90th minute to strike the ball into the net after Emile Heskey's low shot comes back off the inside of the post. A very big three points against title rivals.

NOVEMBER 9 2002

The start of Liverpool's Premiership slump – and the start of Jerzy Dudek's run of poor form. The Reds are just nine minutes away from setting a new Premiership record of games unbeaten since the start of the season when Dudek fumbles a cross and the ball drops for Boro's Gareth Southgate to slot the ball home and inflict Liverpool's first League defeat of the campaign.

NOVEMBER 12 2002

Liverpool's Champions League dreams collapse in a dramatic game in Switzerland against Basel. Needing a win to go through to the second group stages, the Reds aren't at the races in the opening half and go in for the break trailing 3–0. A second half revival with goals from Danny Murphy, Vladimir Smicer and Michael Owen at least restores parity on the night, but it isn't enough to take Liverpool through and they have to content themselves with thoughts of another UEFA Cup run.

DECEMBER 1 2002

Liverpool suffer their first home league defeat of the season when they crash 2–1 to arch rivals Manchester United. After an unexciting first half in which neither side have many chances and goalkeeper Jerzy Dudek looks to be having an easy day, he gifts Diego Forlan a second-half goal before the Uruguayan adds a second shortly after with a well-struck shot. Sami Hyypia gives Liverpool hope six minutes from time but it's too little too late.

DECEMBER 18 2003

Liverpool fans may have had to wait in the snow at Villa Park following a delayed kick-off, but the wait is more than worthwhile as the Reds book their place in the semi-final of the Worthington Cup with an epic 4–3 win over Aston Villa. Danny Murphy is the hero on the night, blasting home in the last minute to deny Villa who had come back from 3–1 down and are on the brink of taking the game into extra-time. One of the great games of the season.

29.01.03

JANUARY 18 2003

The Reds finally end a miserable run of Premiership results with a hard-fought and well-earned 1–0 win at Southampton. Emile Heskey is the hero as he heads home an early free kick to end a run of 11 games without a win for Gerard Houllier's side. "The boys deserved that," says the boss. "I have never lost faith in them."

JANUARY 29 2003

Liverpool salvage a point in a thrilling 2–2 draw with Arsenal at Anfield. Arsenal are quite simply sensational in the first half as Robert Pires gives them the lead, but Liverpool reply before half-time with a goal from John Arne Riise. Dennis Bergkamp regains the lead for Gunners with a deflected second-half shot, but Emile Heskey heads home in stoppage time to earn the Reds a point and put a dent in Arsenal's title hopes.

FEBRUARY 5 2003

A definite low point of the season as Liverpool bow out of the FA Cup against First Division Crystal Palace at Anfield. Following a goalless first game at Selhurst Park, the Reds are odds-on favourites to progress but carelessness in front of goal gives Palace hope and two second-half goals kill off Liverpool's Cup dreams and leave the Eagles ecstatic.

FEBRUARY 20 + 27 2003

Liverpool see off talented French outfit Auxerre in the UEFA Cup to book a quarter-final date with Scottish giants Celtic. Sami Hyypia's strike in France gives the Reds a priceless 1–0 lead to defend at Anfield, and they have little trouble in doing just that as Michael Owen and Danny Murphy give them a 2–0 win on the night, and a 3–0 aggregate victory, to take the Reds into the last eight of the competition.

MARCH 2 2003

Another piece of silverware heads back to Anfield as Liverpool defeat Manchester United 2–0 on a wonderful afternoon in Cardiff. A first-half strike from Steven Gerrard and a late goal from Michael Owen ensure it's Liverpool who are celebrating their second Worthington Cup success in just three years. "This club is all about winning trophies and the players today did themselves, the fans and the club proud," said manager Gerard Houllier.

13.03.03

02.03.03

19.04.03

MARCH 13 + 20 2003

Liverpool lose the 'Battle of Britain' over two legs against Celtic – and so lose the chance to repeat their UEFA Cup triumph of 2001. Following a 1–1 draw at Parkhead, with Emile Heskey on the scoresheet for the Reds, Celtic turn in an impressive second-leg display at Anfield and book their place in the last four with goals from Alan Thompson and John Hartson. "I enjoyed the game," said boss Gerard Houllier. "But I didn't enjoy the result. It's one of these things that happen in football and we have to live with it."

APRIL 19 2003

An under-strength Liverpool team earn local bragging rights following a brilliant 2–1 win at Everton. Deprived of both regular centre-halves, Henchoz and Hyypia, many people are predicting the 'Wayne Rooney show', but Michael Owen proves he's still Merseyside's boy wonder with a great goal in the first half, before David Unsworth levels for the home side from the penalty spot after the break. With victory imperative for Liverpool's Champions League dreams, Danny Murphy is the toast of the red half of the city when he curls home a stunning goal to give all three points to the visitors.

APRIL 21 2003

One of the most dramatic games at Anfield all season as Liverpool make it six points from six over the crucial Easter period to keep their hopes of a top-four finish alive. It isn't looking likely against Charlton though, with the Addicks leading 1–0 with just a few minutes left to play, but Sami Hyypia soon draws Liverpool level before Steven Gerrard scores a goal of individual brilliance in stoppage time to secure a vital, vital win for the Reds.

APRIL 26 2003

Liverpool hit already relegated West Brom for 6 – but it could easily have been 16 at the end of one of the most one-sided games in Premiership history. Michael Owen has a goal-den day – bagging four (including his 100th league goal for Liverpool) and working brilliantly in tandem with strike partner Milan Baros who also helps himself to a couple of goals. "We have been an accident waiting to happen for some weeks now," said beleaguered Baggies boss Gary Megson. "And today it happened big time."

MAY 11 2003

Liverpool's Champions League dreams finally die at Stamford Bridge on the final day of the season. Needing three points to leap over Chelsea into fourth place, the Reds make the perfect start when Sami Hyypia heads home Danny Murphy's free kick. But the home side respond instantly with a headed goal from Marcel Desailly and then take the lead when Jesper Gronkjaer bursts past John Arne Riise inside the area and curls home a terrific left-footed shot. Liverpool get more and more frustrated as the game goes on and Steven Gerrard's season – like his team's – ends on a low note when he is sent off late in the game for two bookable offences.

LIVERPOOL'S PRIDE OF LIONS

DIAO AND DIOUF, ANFIELD'S AFRICAN LIONS, PLAYED A BIG PART IN ROUTING THE FRENCH COCKEREL DURING WORLD CUP 2002 AND NOW THE SENEGALESE DUO ARE MUCH TOUTED AS ANFIELD'S LATEST DOUBLE ACT

S A L I F D I A O

DIAO...

I think I have settled in well at Liverpool. I arrived earlier than expected because the original plan was to wait until last Christmas before coming over here, but then the manager told me he wanted me earlier. I had to adjust quicker than I expected. Liverpool is such a massive club, a mythical club, and so of course it is a pleasure to play here.

My early games in the team were good. I felt as though I was doing well and making my presence felt. English football is so different to anything I had experienced before and it was always going to take some time to fully get used to it. Towards the end of the season I didn't play as much as I would have liked, but I know I have time on my side here and I know that I am still young and learning the game. There is a great spirit among the lads here and I can feel that I am somewhere really special. I want to stay here for as long as possible and to be as successful as possible.

Of course it helps when my friend El Hadji is over here as well. Whenever you move to a new club it is good if there's at least one familiar face who you know well to talk to as you go through the settling-in process. But even if he wasn't here, I wouldn't have had any problems because the lads here are so good and so helpful.

El Hadji can be a real Premiership star. He has everything. I often say to him that, if he had a Brazilian passport, then everyone would always be talking about him because he has all the attributes of a great player.

His only problem – and I mean this in the nicest way – is that he comes from Senegal which isn't renowned for world-class players. He has had a good first season here and I am sure he will only get better and better. ⌖

Liverpool's Senegalese stars El Hadji Diouf and Salif Diao have brought both power and flair to the Reds' squad since Gerard Houllier snapped them up before the start of last season. Diouf, Africa's Player of the Year for two years running, has without doubt added style and panache to the Liverpool team while his fellow countryman Diao has already earned comparisons with Arsenal's Patrick Vieira following a number of impressive displays in Gerard Houllier's midfield. But how are they both settling in at Anfield? And how are they enjoying their new lives on Merseyside? Let's ask them...

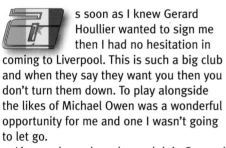

s soon as I knew Gerard Houllier wanted to sign me then I had no hesitation in coming to Liverpool. This is such a big club and when they say they want you then you don't turn them down. To play alongside the likes of Michael Owen was a wonderful opportunity for me and one I wasn't going to let go.

Liverpool are also a huge club in Senegal – and even more so now that Salif and I have come over here. Whenever Liverpool are playing on the television there are people crowded around TV screens wearing red watching us play. It's a great feeling to know we have so much support back home.

I agreed to sign for Liverpool before the World Cup but it was still pleasing to do well in Japan and South Korea because I could show the fans over here what I was capable of. As a country, to get as far as we did in the competition was a great achievement, but I also felt I did quite well on a personal level and that was important for me.

My first season at Liverpool has been a big learning experience. I think any foreign player who goes to England will say they need a period of time to adapt and get used to the new football. The Premiership is a brilliant league. It's very fast and very physical and that would come as a shock to a lot of foreigners. I think I've coped well so far but my best is definitely still to come.

We probably under-achieved as a squad overall last season and we will all be desperate to make up for that this year. It's a big season for us and one we are all looking forward to. ⊕

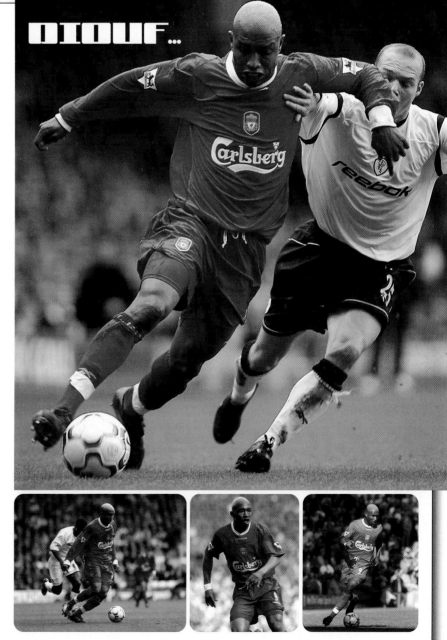

DIOUF...

DOB 27 AUGUST 1973 **NATIONALITY** GERMAN **POSITION** MIDFIELDER **NICKNAME** DIDI
HEIGHT 6' 2 **WEIGHT** 12st 9lbs **SQUAD NUMBER** 16 **PREVIOUS CLUBS** FC WACKER MUNCHEN,
BAYERN MUNCHEN, NEWCASTLE UNITED

DIETMAR HAMANN

1. Why is Didi's name written in Wembley folklore?
2. How old was he when he joined Bayern Munich?
3. How many major trophies did he win in his nine years with Bayern?
4. How much did Liverpool pay for his services?
5. He played in the 2002 World Cup Final. Who was the last Liverpool player before Didi to achieve that feat?
6. What other sport does Didi have a major passion for?
7. Where was he born?
8. Which former Liverpool player signed Didi for Newcastle?
9. At the start of the 1999–2000 season, which injury did he pick up?
10. Who was he talking about when he said: "This boy has everything to be the best midfielder in Europe"?

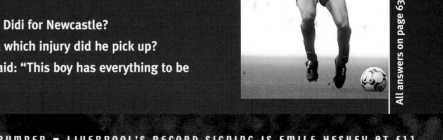

All answers on page 63

+ + + MICHAEL OWEN HAS A DOG CALLED BUMPER ■ LIVERPOOL'S RECORD SIGNING IS EMILE HESKEY AT £11

> 1 Where in the Czech Republic was Vladi born?
>
> 2 Vladi scored on his Liverpool debut – against which team?
>
> 3 In which season did Vladi taste league success in France?
>
> 4 He was brought to Liverpool as a replacement for which player?
>
> 5 How far did he help his country progress in Euro 96?
>
> 6 In what month and year did he sign for Liverpool?
>
> 7 What would he say is his preferred position in the team?
>
> 8 He signed a new contract at the start of the 2002–03 season – for how long?
>
> 9 How far did he progress in the 1996 UEFA Cup with Slavia Prague?
>
> 10 Has he made more than 50 appearances for his country? Yes or no?

DOB 24 MAY 1973 **NATIONALITY** CZECH **POSITION** MIDFIELDER **NICKNAME** VLADI **HEIGHT** 5' 10
WEIGHT 11st 13lbs **SQUAD NUMBER** 7 **PREVIOUS CLUBS** SLAVIA PRAGUE, LENS

VLADIMIR SMICER

T
H
E

L
I
V
E
R
P
O
O
L

W
A
Y

THE LIVERPOOL WAY

SINCE ARRIVING AT ANFIELD FIVE YEARS AGO GERARD HOULLIER HAS RID THE REDS OF THEIR UNFORTUNATE 'SPICE BOYS' IMAGE AND HAS GONE ABOUT RESTRUCTURING THE CLUB AND THE PLAYING STAFF IN A WAY THAT BEFITS LIVERPOOL FC'S GLORIOUS HISTORY

There's a sign on Houllier's office wall at Melwood which perfectly describes the qualities he looks for in each of his players. It says simply:
  Respect
  Be a winner
  Always think team first
  Be a top pro

"I think these are all vital qualities if you want to achieve success," says the manager. "You must always respect the opposition. Always. Complacency is something I won't tolerate at my club. It can be like a cancer and can eat away at you. I won't have that and I insist that all of my players always take their opponents seriously and give them the respect they deserve.

"You must want to be a winner to play for Liverpool. This club has built its history on winning trophies and the fans are happiest when we're bringing silverware to the club. But to be a winner you must want to work hard. You can never programme success, but you can prepare for it and that is what we do at Liverpool. I want players who want to achieve and who want to get to the top.

"But you can't do that with a team of individuals. They must work together as a team and work hard for each other. If Michael Owen wins the European Player of the Year award, then it's because he has a good team around him who can create the chances for him to score the goals. Team work is very important in

the modern game and you will only be successful if you have a group of players who will work as hard as they possibly can for each other.

"It's important that you are a good person as well and a good professional. Footballers are role models for kids and when you look at your idol on the TV you want to see a good person. It's always important when thinking about bringing new players to the club that you do your homework on their temperament and character as much as on their ability. You need a harmonious unit if you hope to win trophies.

"This club has a wonderful history and it is our job now to keep that going into the future. Liverpool has a special way of doing things and there is definitely a special bond between the players and the supporters. That means a lot to me.

"I'll never forget when we won the UEFA Cup in Dortmund and the players stood in a line in front of the fans and we all sang 'You'll Never Walk Alone'. That was a very special experience and one we shall all remember for a long, long time.

"Even last season when we went through a bad patch I was heartened by the messages of support I got from the fans. They were telling me to keep going and not to get too down. This club is special and I feel privileged to be here.

"We celebrate together when things are good and we suffer together when things are bad. The Liverpool way is special." ⊕

Gerard Houllier with the UEFA Cup, 2001

Murphy and Owen celebrate Worthington winner

Rush and Johnston with the European Cup, 1984

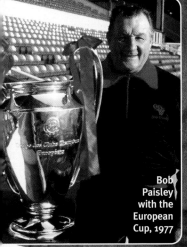
Bob Paisley with the European Cup, 1977

Joyful Liverpool after winning the FA Cup at Wembley in 1992

Liverpool in Rome , 1977

LIST OF HONOURS

CHAMPIONS

1900–01 • 1905–06 • 1921–22 • 1922–23
1946–47 • 1963–64 • 1965–66 • 1972–73
1975–76 • 1976–77 • 1978–79 • 1979–80
1981–82 • 1982–83 • 1983–84 •
1985–86 • 1987–88 • 1989–90

DIVISION 2 WINNERS

1893–94 • 1895–96 • 1904–05 • 1961–62

FA CUP WINNERS

1964–65 • 1973–74 • 1985–86 • 1988–89
1991–92 • 2000–2001

LEAGUE CUP WINNERS

1980–81 • 1981–82 • 1982–83
1983–84 • 1994–95 • 2000–01
2002–03

CHARITY SHIELD WINNERS

1964* • 1965* • 1966 • 1974 • 1976 •
1977* 1979 • 1980 • 1982 • 1986* • 1988
• 1989 • 1990* • 2001
* TROPHY SHARED

EUROPEAN CUP WINNERS

1976–77 • 1977–78 • 1980–81 • 1983–84

UEFA CUP WINNERS

1972–73 • 1975–76 • 2000–01

EUROPEAN SUPER CUP WINNERS

1977 • 2001

Keeping

The contest for the goalkeeper's jersey at Anfield has been an intriguing sideshow to an up-and-down season for the Reds, with both keepers demonstrating on numerous occasions that they possess the quality and desire to hold down a regular place in the team.

Dudek – outstanding for the Reds in his debut season last year – began the campaign in equally fine form before a series of mistakes eventually cost him his place and presented Kirkland with a chance to show what he could do.

The England Under-21 goalkeeper was proving to be a more than able deputy and was well on his way to being fast-tracked into Sven-Goran Eriksson's full England squad before disaster struck at Crystal Palace and he sustained a knee injury which sidelined him for the rest of the season.

That gave Dudek another chance to prove his early-season wobbles were a thing of the past – and left Kirkland with ambitions for club and country temporarily on hold.

Dudek grabbed his chance with both hands and a Man of the Match performance in the Worthington Cup Final was all the proof anyone needed that the Polish star was back to his breathtaking best.

Despite the intense battle for the number one jersey, each goalkeeper holds the other in incredibly high esteem, with Kirkland saying Dudek is one of the best in the world and Dudek repaying the compliment by insisting Kirkland has all the attributes to be England's first-choice goalkeeper for years to come.

It all adds up to a healthy dilemma for manager Gerard Houllier, and he insists that sort of selection headache is something every boss would enjoy.

Houllier says: "We are fortunate at this club that we have two top-class goalkeepers. When we decided to sign them both on the same day, I explained the situation to them and said that Jerzy would be the number one.

"He did brilliantly for us during his first season and won us many points. Then for a spell this season his game dipped and it was the right decision to give Chris Kirkland a run. He was doing really well until he picked up the injury, but I never had any doubts that Jerzy would come back and show that what happened to him in the early part of the season was now firmly behind him."

ENEMIES AS THEY BATTLE FOR LIVERPOOL'S NUMBER ONE SPOT. IN FACT, THEY ARE THE BEST OF MATES!

friends

Dudek admits his form let him down in the run-up to Christmas and he fully supported his manager's decision to take him out of the firing line.

The Polish star says: "I wasn't feeling good about my game. I was finding it hard to concentrate and I wasn't right mentally. I needed a rest. I had played a full season and then went to the World Cup and I think it all added up and took its toll.

"It was a bad experience for me to make some big mistakes, especially in the league game with Manchester United at Anfield, but the club stood by me and supported me and I thank them very much for that.

"The rest did me good. I worked very hard in training and gradually I could feel my game coming back together. That was important for me.

"Obviously in my absence Chris came in and did a good job, which I knew he would. He is a great goalkeeper and is at an age where he is only going to get better. He has plenty of time to learn and he will be England goalkeeper for a long time, I'm sure of that."

Kirkland could be forgiven for believing footballing fate is cruelly conspiring against him. After working so hard to finally get his chance at Anfield, it now seems as though he will have to start all over again to dislodge Dudek from the Liverpool goal – but he remains philosophical about the whole situation.

He says: "What happened to me in terms of the injury was just part and parcel of football. That's the way it goes at times in this game.

"As soon as the clash took place between me and Dele Adebola at Crystal Palace, I knew it was a bad injury because I was in so much pain. I was down for a few days but then picked myself up and concentrated on getting fit as quickly as I could.

"It was a relief to be told I didn't need an operation, but I've had to work to a strict rehab programme devised by a doctor in America, Richard Steadman.

"It's going to be a challenge for me to get another chance in the team, but at a club the size of Liverpool nobody has a divine right to be playing and it's only right that we should all be fighting for an opportunity.

"As far as I am concerned, Jerzy is one of the best goalkeepers in the world but I knew the situation before I signed and I knew I might have to be patient. I've had a taste of the first team now and really enjoyed it. I want more of the same in the future but I'm prepared to work hard and wait for my chance."

CHRIS KIRKLAND

MICHAEL OWEN

DOB 14 DECEMBER 1979 **NATIONALITY** ENGLISH **POSITION** STRIKER **NICKNAME** MO
HEIGHT 5' 8 **WEIGHT** 10st 9lbs **SQUAD NUMBER** 10 **PREVIOUS CLUBS** NONE

1 Where was Michael Owen born?

2 Against which club did he score his first goal for Liverpool?

3 Against which country did he score his first goal for England?

4 Which two countries did he score against in the 2002 World Cup?

5 In December 2002, he was awarded the *Ballon d'Or*. What for?

6 Against which team did he notch his 100th League goal? (It was last season)

7 Why was his goal against Auxerre at Anfield in February 2003 significant?

8 Which Premiership club has Michael scored most goals against so far?

9 In which city did he score that wonder goal for England v Argentina in 1998?

10 Which clubs did Michael's dad play professional football for?

All answers on page 63

+ + + JERZY DUDEK SAYS HE WOULD HAVE BEEN A MINER HAD HE NOT FOUND A CAREER IN FOOTBALL + + + JAMIE CARRAGHER

1. How many League Cup finals has Emile played in?
2. Why was his transfer from Leicester to Anfield so historic?
3. In which year did Emile make his debut for Leicester?
4. After how many games did he score his first goal for Liverpool?
5. Against which team did he score his first hat-trick for Liverpool?
6. How many goals did he score in the 2002 World Cup?
7. Why were Leicester fans so grateful to their former idol during 2003?
8. How many Cup Finals has Emile scored in for Liverpool?
9. Who does Emile base his famous DJ goalscoring celebration on?
10. How many goals did he score during his first full season at Anfield?

DOB 11 JANUARY 1978 **NATIONALITY** ENGLISH **POSITION** STRIKER **NICKNAME** BRUNO
HEIGHT 6' 2 **WEIGHT** 13st 12lbs **SQUAD NUMBER** 8 **PREVIOUS CLUBS** LEICESTER CITY

EMILE HESKEY

STEVEN GERRARD

DOB 30 MAY 1980 **NATIONALITY** ENGLISH **POSITION** MIDFIELDER **NICKNAME** STEVIE G
HEIGHT 6' 1 **WEIGHT** 12st 6lbs **SQUAD NUMBER** 17 **PREVIOUS CLUBS** NONE

> 1 Which injury prevented Gerrard going to the World Cup in 2002?
> 2 Against which team did he make his Liverpool debut?
> 3 Name the five finals he played in prior to this season.
> 4 When did he score his first England goal?
> 5 What was the final score in that match?
> 6 How many goals has he scored against Manchester United in his career so far?
> 7 Which England manager gave him his first chance at international level?
> 8 Which squad number did he wear before taking over the number 17 shirt?
> 9 Has he ever captained Liverpool in his career to date?
> 10 Where in Liverpool was he born?

All answers on page 63

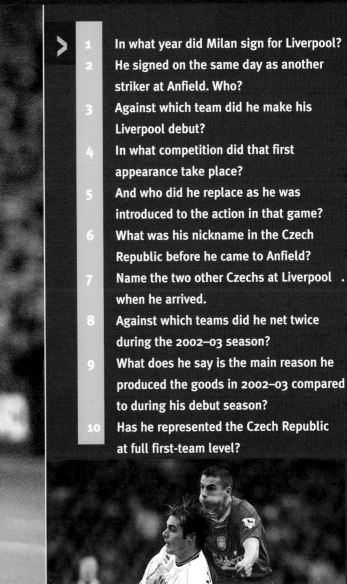

1. In what year did Milan sign for Liverpool?
2. He signed on the same day as another striker at Anfield. Who?
3. Against which team did he make his Liverpool debut?
4. In what competition did that first appearance take place?
5. And who did he replace as he was introduced to the action in that game?
6. What was his nickname in the Czech Republic before he came to Anfield?
7. Name the two other Czechs at Liverpool when he arrived.
8. Against which teams did he net twice during the 2002–03 season?
9. What does he say is the main reason he produced the goods in 2002–03 compared to during his debut season?
10. Has he represented the Czech Republic at full first-team level?

DOB 28 OCTOBER 1981 **NATIONALITY** CZECH **POSITION** STRIKER **NICKNAME** MILAN **HEIGHT** 6'0
WEIGHT 13st 2lbs **SQUAD NUMBER** 5 **PREVIOUS CLUBS** BANIK OSTRAVA

MILAN BAROS

S
T
E
V
E
N
G
E
R
R
A
R
D

'Stevie G'

STEVEN GERRARD IS A LIFELONG LIVERPOOL FAN AND HE CONTINUES TO STAMP HIS MARK ON BOTH CLUB AND COUNTRY. BUT IS HE A FUTURE ENGLAND CAPTAIN?

England captain David Beckham may have no plans to hand over the armband just yet – and no doubt Michael Owen would be next in line even if he had – but at some point in Steven Gerrard's footballing career surely there can't be much doubt that he will enjoy the ultimate honour of skippering his country.

The Liverpool midfielder continues to go from strength to strength as he proves, game after game, that he is, without doubt, the best young midfield talent in the country.

It's often said that when Gerrard plays well then Liverpool play well. His commanding performances from the heart of midfield often help drive the Reds on to victory, while his displays for the national side have played a huge part in England's upturn in fortunes since the appointment of Sven-Goran Eriksson.

His club manager Gerard Houllier has never made any secret of his admiration for the Whiston-born star and has often handed him the honour of captaining Liverpool whenever

Stepping up: Gerrard has realised his dream of playing for his boyhood club and now has a bright future for his country

Sami Hyypia has been missing.

"Stevie is a great leader," says Houllier. "He has shown that he can be a great leader for the present and for the future.

"He has great energy to his game and he is only going to get better and better because, don't forget, he is still very young. I like the way his game is developing and I have liked his performances for us since he came into the side.

"He always wants to learn about the game and he is prepared to listen to advice from our coaching staff. There's no doubt he has the talent to make a good career for himself in the game but I would say his best is still to come."

That is a statement Gerrard completely agrees with as he looks forward to helping the Reds enjoy more success over the coming years.

He says: "This is my club. I have always been a Liverpool fan and so to get the chance to play for them is fantastic for me. I don't take anything for granted. I know how lucky I am to be in this position and I know I'm living the dream of so many

kids in Liverpool.

"I've worked hard to get where I am today but there is still a tremendous amount of hard work lying ahead of me. I'm happy to make the sacrifices you need to make as a footballer because the rewards are great.

"I think I've done well since the gaffer gave me a chance in the side at a young age and I certainly don't feel as though I have let anyone down. I've had up and down patches in terms of form but that would be the case for any youngster in the game."

It was during one spell last season when Gerrard needed to seek advice and solace from the club's management staff as he felt his game falling apart at the seams – and the harder he tried to put it right, the worse it got.

STEVIE'S STATS FOR CLUB AND COUNTRY UP TO MAY 2003

1ST TEAM GAMES	193
1ST TEAM GOALS	22
ENGLAND CAPS	15
ENGLAND GOALS	2

He recalls: "That was a bad spell for me early on last season. I don't know what was going wrong but I just couldn't seem to get my act together. I would try things and they wouldn't come off and then I would try even harder the next time. And the harder I tried the worse it was. It was a really bad time for me and I spoke on several occasions to the manager and coaching staff. The advice and help they gave me was first class and it wasn't too long before I felt my form coming back again.

"I think I finished last season strongly and felt really good as far as personal performances go. I felt I was contributing to the team and helping us get the results."

Gerrard is almost certainly one of the 'untouchables' at Anfield – one of those players who Gerard Houllier wouldn't sell for any money. And, in the eyes of many people, he's just as important to country as he is to club.

"I love playing for England," he said. "I was absolutely gutted to miss the World Cup in the summer but I knew I had to because of my injury. Watching that on the television wasn't a nice experience because every player wants to play for their country on the highest possible stage.

"I'm pleased that the England manager has kept faith with me and kept me in his squads. That means a lot. Working in that environment with the best players in the country can only help me keep improving as a footballer.

"I want to win things with Liverpool and I want to win things with England. And I think I can achieve both aims. Being a footballer is all I ever wanted to do and I'm definitely going to give everything to make sure I have as successful a career as possible."

DOB 15 JANUARY 1981 **NATIONALITY** SENEGALESE **POSITION** STRIKER **NICKNAME** THE SERIAL KILLER **HEIGHT** 5'9 **WEIGHT** 12st 3lbs **SQUAD NUMBER** 9 **PREVIOUS CLUBS** ASC KAANI GUI, SOCHEAUX, RENNES, LENS

EL HADJI DIOUF

1. How much did Gerard Houllier pay for his services?
2. What tattoo does he have on his body?
3. In which competition did Diouf score his first goal for Liverpool?
4. Which Liverpool player does Diouf say is helping him to learn English?
5. Which major award did he win in 2001 and 2002?
6. How far did he help his country progress in the 2002 World Cup?
7. How many clubs did he play for before he joined the Reds?
8. Where did his former club Lens finish in the French league before he left?
9. How far did he help Senegal to progress in the 2002 African Nations Cup?
10. How many games did he play in European competition during his first season at Liverpool?

All answers on page 63

> **1** Against which country did Salif score in the 2002 World Cup?
>
> **2** Give a reason why he will remember that same game with regret.
>
> **3** How many seasons did he spend playing for Monaco?
>
> **4** What silverware did he pick up during his time in France?
>
> **5** Against which team did he score his first goal for Liverpool?
>
> **6** What positions did he play for Liverpool during his first season at Anfield?
>
> **7** Which former Fulham manager was his coach at Monaco?
>
> **8** Why was he surprised to be at Liverpool at the start of the 2002–03 season?
>
> **9** How much did Gerard Houllier pay for his services?
>
> **10** What was the name of the Senegal coach who persuaded Diao to play for his country after he had previously refused?

DOB 10 FEBRUARY 1977 **NATIONALITY** SENEGALESE **POSITION** MIDFIELDER **NICKNAME** THE NINJA
HEIGHT 6' 1 **WEIGHT** 13st **SQUAD NUMBER** 21 **PREVIOUS CLUBS** EPINAL, MONACO, SEDAN

SALIF DIAO

BAROS
SUPERSTAR IN THE MAKING

THE YOUNG CZECH STRIKER IS DETERMINED TO MAKE HIS MARK AT ANFIELD AND GERARD HOULLIER HAS EVERY CONFIDENCE IN HIS ABILITY TO DO SO

When Milan Baros netted two brilliant goals for Liverpool early last season, manager Gerard Houllier admitted even his own coaching staff had entertained doubts over whether the Czech youngster would make the grade in the Premiership. Following a disappointing debut season, during which Baros failed to make the impact Kopites everywhere were hoping for, the young striker returned for training last summer leaner and fitter than ever before and desperate to prove he couldn't be considered a big-money Anfield flop.

It didn't take long for him to prove he had what it takes to be a success in the Premiership as his powerful and energetic performances in the Liverpool front line endeared him to the hearts of Reds' fans everywhere – much to the delight of the boss.

Houllier says: "By his own admission, Milan didn't have a great first few months with us. He was in a new environment, he couldn't speak the language and he struggled to get to grips with the English way of playing.

"I think even my own coaching staff thought I had made a mistake by signing him, even though they didn't say that to me directly. I had scouted Milan on a number of occasions before we signed him and I knew what the boy was capable of. He had scored goals in Czech football as well as for his country and I was always confident he could do it here.

"But last season was an important one for him. It was his chance to show he had what it takes and I was delighted with his attitude when he came back for pre-season training. He had lost several kilos over the summer and I knew he really

meant business. He was strong and sharp in training and I knew he would have a big part to play in our future."

Baros may have taken a while to come to terms with life in England and with life in the Premiership, but his Anfield team-mate and fellow countryman Vladimir Smicer never had any doubts he would be a success.

Smicer says: "I have known Milan for a long time and I know all about his qualities. He is a great young striker and a player who will always score goals.

"After his first season he was a bit down because he knew he hadn't done himself justice. I don't know whether he expected to just walk into the team and stay there, but I explained to him that was never going to be the case at a club of this size.

"I never had any doubts he would prove himself here though. I have played with him many, many times for club and country and he is definitely a great player for today and for the future. He just needed to get his head sorted out and to realise that it would take a lot of hard work to succeed at Liverpool, but he has done that now and I really believe he is going to have a very good career here.

"He has scored goals now for Liverpool, he has put in some great displays and the fans have really taken to him. That's half the battle won in many ways. Now he just needs to keep working hard because he already has the natural

talent, there's no doubt about that."

But what about Baros himself? How much happier is he feeling now he has proved himself capable of scoring goals in one of the best leagues in world football?

"I'm happy at the moment," he says. "It was difficult for me at first because I wanted to play more, but I soon realised that I was going to have to work a lot harder to get a chance in the team here.

"There are world-class players throughout the squad at Liverpool, and so the competition is very hard. But I know I can do well in the Premiership and I think the manager knows I won't let him down when a chance comes along for me.

"I love the relationship I have with the fans here. They are always singing my name and I can feel that they are right behind me. That means such a lot when you are a young player looking to do well in a different country.

"I am improving all the time and I think it will be a few years yet before I hit my very best form. I'm working every day in training with some of the best strikers around and I can only learn from them and improve.

"My aim now is to keep improving as I have been doing over recent months and to take my opportunities in the team when they come along. I feel as though I have made a good start to my Liverpool career but I still have a lot more to offer in the future."

"HE IS A GREAT YOUNG STRIKER AND A PLAYER WHO WILL ALWAYS SCORE GOALS"

MILAN'S STATS FOR CLUB AND COUNTRY UP TO MAY 2003	
1ST TEAM GAMES	43
1ST TEAM GOALS	12
CZECH CAPS	15
CZECH GOALS	6

NEW PLAYERS ARE THE LIFEBLOOD OF LIVERPOOL FC AND CHIEF SCOUT, ALEX MILLER, IS A MAN WITH A MISSION. HE TRAVELS THE GLOBE IN HIS SEARCH FOR THE BEST YOUNG TALENT WORLD FOOTBALL HAS TO OFFER

With Craig Brown and Scotland

CATCH THEM YOUNG

PAUL EATON: Alex, first of all please explain your role and how you got the job?

ALEX MILLER: I first met with Gerard Houllier when he worked for UEFA during Euro 96 and he was trying to ascertain the different methods countries were using in training. Gerard came to watch Scotland train, so he saw me coaching. When I was manager at Aberdeen, I asked him if he could tell me

about the French youth development system. He told me how it was structured and what they did, and it was very informative. When he arrived at Anfield, he told me he had this role in mind for me at Liverpool and asked me to come and help the staff. I said yes. My role here is coaching and working with the younger players, together with Hughie McAuley, and I always watch the opposition for their tactics and to see

their team formation. I pass on the information to the coaching staff. When we are scouting a player we have a structured organisation which I am in charge of. We look at the players and when we make final decisions I recommend to the manager, on behalf of the scouting department, that we should sign him. Gerard will then send a senior member of staff, or go himself, to watch the player.

1976: scoring from the spot for Rangers

PE: Was it an easy decision for you to come here?

AM: This is a massive club. I spent 17 years at Glasgow Rangers which is another big club. This club is run along the right lines. What we have here is a collective team unit and everyone – from the lad that does the kit up to the manager – is very supportive of everyone else. All of our focus is on getting the best results for Liverpool Football Club.

PE: How impressive was Gerard Houllier when you first met him?

AM: He is very knowledgeable about the game. He is a bit like myself – a football alcoholic! Gerard has a TV channel that picks up all the football you can get. He is also a good delegator which is important at this level. He lets you get on with your job as long as you keep him informed. It's important for him as a manager of the club to know everything that's going on as he is the guy who takes the club in a certain direction and we have to give him our support.

PE: As far as your job is concerned, it's safe to say you rack up a lot of road miles and air miles...

AM: It can of course be quite tiring at times but how gruelling it ends up depends on the times and dates of games. I was up in Manchester the other week for a 12.15 pm kick-off then off to the airport for a 3.40 pm flight to Amsterdam. In Amsterdam I had to take a two-hour car journey to watch a match. Then on the Sunday morning, I flew into London to watch Charlton. So it can be non-stop.

PE: Do you enjoy the travelling side?

AM: I keep myself fit and active which helps. Sometimes travel can come in blocks and then you are really busy; sometimes it eases off. We are actively looking all the time for the best young talent in Europe and world football, so we have to be prepared to do distances.

PE: You must have been to most places around the world then with this job?

AM: I've been to South America and all over the world. The only place I've not been to much is Africa.

PE: Is it a job you enjoy?

AM: As part of the job I get to do coaching and that is something I really like doing. I have the top coaching licence and I would say that being able to coach is my forte. My specialist area is tactics: how to beat and break down the opposition and analysing strengths and weaknesses.

PE: Just as importantly, you are heavily involved in the process leading to many of Gerard Houllier's signings?

AM: That's correct though sometimes my recommendation has been not to sign someone, but the boss fancied him so he went ahead and signed him anyway. The most important thing from a scouting department's point of view is to know about the players coming through. We don't want a young player signing for another top club without us having background reports on him. That would mean I wasn't doing my job properly, but, touch wood, up until now we haven't missed many. We've a good record of bringing players to the club.

PE: Do you have to watch certain players more than once before deciding you want to recommend them?

AM: Any player can have a bad game so it's folly to just watch him once. We will watch any player at the very least a couple of times but it's important on that first visit that the player excites you if you are to come back. His movement has to be good and his game intelligence – what he is trying to do, the pictures in his head – his pace and his passing have to be impressive. Speed and technique are a very important part of modern-day football. If you don't have the pace, then you need to be an exceptional player to make it.

PE: It sounds like you don't get to see too many Liverpool games with all this travelling?

AM: No, unfortunately I don't. You are always travelling often in strange places where you have to have your wits about you. And they don't lay on transport to and from the ground. You are out on your own. It's easy to get a taxi to the stadium but difficult to get one back to the hotel. Most of the hotels we try and pick are by the airport because I normally have to get an early flight to get back to training.

PE: When you are away and Liverpool are playing, do you try and find the result and see how they are playing?

AM: Oh, all the time. The staff communicate regularly with me by telephone, so I speak to Phil, Sammy or the manager and tell them briefly how the game I have been watching has gone, and in turn they will tell me about theirs. I always try and keep in touch as best as I can, wherever I end up in the world.

JOHN ARNE RIISE

DOB 24 SEPTEMBER 1980 **NATIONALITY** NORWEGIAN **POSITION** DEFENDER **NICKNAME** GINGER
HEIGHT 6'1 **WEIGHT** 11st **SQUAD NUMBER** 18 **PREVIOUS CLUBS** AALESUND, MONACO

> 1 During which game did Riise first perform his now famous goal celebration of taking his shirt off?
> 2 What is the name of his mother, who used to be his agent?
> 3 Which Premiership club did he turn down to sign for Liverpool?
> 4 How much did his transfer cost Liverpool?
> 5 Why was his first goal for Liverpool so special?
> 6 Against which team did he score his first Anfield goal?
> 7 What award did he win from his native Norway in 2001?
> 8 How many goals did he score during his first season at Liverpool?
> 9 Why was the 2003 Worthington Cup final extra special for Riise?
> 10 Who is his closest friend in the Liverpool squad?

All answers on page 63

> 1   From which club did Liverpool sign Bruno?
>
> 2   What did he win with Lille in 2000?
>
> 3   Which English team did he score against in the Champions League in the 2001–02 season?
>
> 4   Which French club did he turn down to sign for Liverpool?
>
> 5   Against which team did he make his Anfield debut?
>
> 6   Against which team did he score his first Liverpool goal?
>
> 7   Has he won a full international cap with his country?
>
> 8   With which Chelsea star does he share family connections?
>
> 9   Who is his all-time footballing hero?
>
> 10   What's the name of his brother who plays in the French league?

DOB 10 MAY 1978 **NATIONALITY** FRENCH **POSITION** MIDFIELDER **NICKNAME** BRUNO
HEIGHT 6'1 **WEIGHT** 13st 3lbs **SQUAD NUMBER** 28 **PREVIOUS CLUBS** LENS, RACING CLUB
PARIS, LILLE

BRUNO CHEYROU

HUGH McAULEY
THE FUTURE LOOKS BRIGHT

RESERVE TEAM BOSS HUGH McAULEY IS HAPPY THAT ONCE AGAIN THIS YEAR SOME OF HIS YOUNG CHARGES HAVE EDGED EVER CLOSER TOWARDS ACHIEVING THEIR DREAM OF FIRST-TEAM FOOTBALL AT ANFIELD

H

U

G

H

M

C

A

U

L

E

Y

> Over the past twelve months Hugh McAuley has seen Neil Mellor, Jon Otsemobor and John Welsh all play first team football for the Reds, while several others have improved markedly and closed in on living the dream of every kid on Merseyside.

"It's been a good year for us," says Liverpool's reserve team manager. "The main aim of football at our level is always to develop players for the first team. That's our goal and is what we're striving for throughout the season.

"Of course we want to win games as well. This is Liverpool Football Club and so of course winning is important, but at reserve level it's not the be all and end all. Every day in training myself and the other coaches are looking for the lads to improve, to work harder and to take on board the advice we are giving them.

"If they're with us at Melwood or in our reserve team, then they have the ability. It's then just a question of us nurturing them and developing them to the standard required to get into our first team. Of course, the standard needed is exceptionally high and not all of them will make it, but we will give them every chance and they know they are learning in the best possible environment and with the best possible facilities."

If Liverpool's youngsters need any proof that youth is given a chance at Anfield then they need only look at the array of stars who have progressed through the club's Academy programme and earned themselves big reputations in the footballing world.

Michael Owen, Steven Gerrard, Robbie Fowler, Jamie Carragher, David Thompson and Steve McManaman are just a small selection of former Anfield youth players who have gone on to enjoy great careers in the game, and Hugh insists the current crop of Anfield youngsters can take heart from that impressive list.

He says: "This is a big club and everyone understands that the manager and staff will always be looking to bring in players and sometimes spend big money when necessary.

"But there are enough examples in the past of players who have come through the ranks and played first-team football here to tell today's youngsters that if they're good enough then they will have a chance. Obviously they will need to be of a certain standard before the manager will include them in his plans, but we're happy that some lads have had a chance over the last year or so.

"Neil Mellor is the one people have been talking about because of his performances and goalscoring record

WELSH

OTSEMOBOR

MELLOR

at reserve team level. He has done exceptionally well and has really improved over the last eighteen months.

"He is a natural goalscorer. He will always find space in the penalty area and will always create chances for himself. He may have an awkward style about him, but he is very effective and nobody can argue with his scoring statistics. They are remarkable really.

"He has enjoyed a taste of first-team football now and will no doubt want more of the same in the future. He's signed a new contract here so clearly the manager thinks highly of him and that should be a real boost to his confidence.

"We have a lot of good strikers at the club and so he knows it's going to be difficult to force his way in on a regular basis, but if he keeps improving at the rate he has over the last couple of seasons then he will have every chance.

"There are other lads who have done well. Jon Otsemobor was doing well for the reserves when he got a chance in the Worthington Cup last season and he acquitted himself well at right-back. John Welsh, who has been very consistent for a long time, also played in a first-team game, so that experience will stand him in good stead for the future."

Hugh is thoroughly enjoying his role combining coaching duties with taking charge of the reserve team – and providing a valuable link between the staff and players at training ground Melwood and the Academy operation a few miles away in Kirkby.

He says: "I spent so long working at the Academy so it's only natural that I'm a kind of link now between the two places. It's important all of the staff know about the young players and about who is or isn't doing well.

"I love working for this club and it's a real honour for me to be coaching the reserve team along with Alex Miller. It's a relatively new experience for me and one I am really enjoying.

"If I work with a player week after week and then see that player improving in match situations then it is a bit of a thrill. It's always the boys who deserve the credit for what they achieve because they're the ones who have to make the sacrifices and who have to put the work in, but it does give the coaches a boost when they see their work paying off."

And with the quality within the club's youth ranks remaining well up to standard, there should be many more reasons for the Reds' coaching staff to give themselves a well-earned pat on the back over the coming months and years. It'll be fascinating to see who makes the first team. ⊕

DJIMI TRAORE

DOB 1 MARCH 1980 **NATIONALITY** FRENCH **POSITION** DEFENDER **NICKNAME** JIMMY
HEIGHT 6' 3 **WEIGHT** 12st 8lbs **SQUAD NUMBER** 30 **PREVIOUS CLUBS** LAVAL

> 1. In which month and year did Djimi Traore sign for Liverpool?
> 2. At which football league ground did he make his Liverpool debut?
> 3. Against which side did he make his Premiership debut?
> 4. When did he sign a new four year Liverpool contract?
> 5. Where did he spend the 2001–02 season?
> 6. Which former Liverpool staff member did he team up with there?
> 7. Who said of him: "He's a player with great potential and is a real player for the future"?
> 8. Against which team did he score his first goal for Liverpool?
> 9. How many appearances has he made for the French national team?
> 10. What does he say is his favoured position in the team?

All answers on page 63

1. Who is Neil's famous footballing father?
2. How many goals did he score at youth level during the 2001–02 season?
3. Against which side did he make his first appearance for the first team?
4. Who were the opposition when he played for the first time in a competitive fixture?
5. Did he score in that game?
6. On which ground did he score his first Liverpool goal?
7. In which city was he born?
8. Which team was he with as a schoolboy before coming to Liverpool?
9. Who is his footballing idol?
10. When did he graduate to Melwood to start training with the first team?

DOB 4 NOVEMBER 1982 **NATIONALITY** ENGLISH **POSITION** STRIKER **NICKNAME** GERD
HEIGHT 6'0 **WEIGHT** 13st 7lbs **SQUAD NUMBER** 33 **PREVIOUS CLUBS** NONE

NEIL MELLOR

WISE WORDS

THERE HAVE BEEN PLENTY OF CHARACTERS AT ANFIELD OVER THE YEARS AND THEIR

IF EVERTON WERE PLAYING AT THE BOTTOM OF MY GARDEN I'D DRAW THE CURTAINS.
— *Bill Shankly*

THE KOP'S EXCLUSIVE, AN INSTITUTION, AND IF YOU'RE A MEMBER OF THE KOP YOU FEEL YOU'RE A MEMBER OF A SOCIETY, YOU'VE GOT THOUSANDS OF FRIENDS AROUND YOU AND THEY'RE UNITED AND LOYAL.
— *Bill Shankly*

I WAS THE BEST MANAGER IN BRITAIN BECAUSE I WAS NEVER DEVIOUS OR CHEATED ANYONE. I'D BREAK MY WIFE'S LEGS IF I PLAYED AGAINST HER, BUT I'D NEVER CHEAT HER.
— *Bill Shankly*

I WANT TO BUILD A TEAM THAT'S INVINCIBLE, SO THEY'LL HAVE TO SEND A TEAM FROM MARS TO BEAT US.
— *Bill Shankly*

TOMMY SMITH WOULD START A RIOT IN A GRAVEYARD.
— *Bill Shankly*

TAKE THAT POOF BANDAGE OFF AND WHAT DO YOU MEAN YOU'VE HURT <u>YOUR</u> KNEE? IT'S LIVERPOOL'S KNEE.
— *Bill Shankly talking to Tommy Smith*

I HAVE ONLY FELT LIKE THIS ONCE BEFORE, AND THAT WAS WHEN MY FATHER DIED, BECAUSE BILL WAS LIKE A SECOND FATHER TO ME.
— *Kevin Keegan on Bill Shankly's death*

IT'S NOT ABOUT THE LONG BALL OR THE SHORT BALL, IT'S ABOUT THE RIGHT BALL.
— *Bob Paisley*

MIND, I'VE BEEN HERE DURING THE BAD TIMES TOO. ONE YEAR WE CAME SECOND.
— *Bob Paisley*

I'VE BEEN ON THIS PLANET FOR 45 YEARS, AND HAVE SUPPORTED LIVERPOOL FOR 42 OF THEM.
— *Roy Evans in 1994*

ANFIELD WITHOUT EUROPEAN FOOTBALL IS LIKE A BANQUET WITHOUT WINE.
— *Roy Evans*

THERE'S NO NOISE LIKE THE ANFIELD NOISE AND I LOVE IT.
— *Ian St John*

WORDS OF WIT AND WISDOM ARE BEING HANDED DOWN FROM GENERATION TO GENERATION

LIVERPOOL FOOTBALL CLUB IS ALL ABOUT WINNING THINGS AND BEING A SOURCE OF PRIDE TO OUR FANS. IT HAS NO OTHER PURPOSE.
— *Chairman*
David Moores

THE CHIEF EXECUTIVE PETER ROBINSON AND I HAD JUST SAT DOWN AT OUR FORTNIGHTLY MEETING WITH THE MANAGER WHEN HE CAME OUT AND SAID HE WANTED TO FINISH. I JOKINGLY SAID: "THIS AFTERNOON?" AND HE SAID: "YES."
— *Noel White on Kenny*
Dalglish's resignation

TO BE THE BEST YOU HAVE TO FORGET THE PARTYING AND CONCENTRATE ALL YOUR ENERGIES ON THE FOOTBALL.
— *Michael Owen*

IT'S NOT NICE GOING TO THE SUPERMARKET AND THE WOMAN AT THE TILL'S THINKING, "DODGY KEEPER!"
— *David James in 1997*

MY FAVOURITE PLAYER IN THE WHOLE WORLD IS MICHAEL OWEN.
— *Pele*

OUR METHODS ARE SO EASY, SOMETIMES PLAYERS DON'T UNDERSTAND THEM AT FIRST.
— *Joe Fagan*

MY PHILOSOPHY IS THAT THE CLUB IS MORE IMPORTANT THAN ANYONE.
— *Gerard Houllier*

WHEN YOU HAVE A LIVERPOOL SHIRT ON YOUR BACK AS PART OF THE SQUAD, YOU WILL DO ANYTHING TO MAKE SURE YOU PRESERVE WHAT IT STANDS FOR.
— *Gerard Houllier*

IF HE STAYS OUT OF NIGHT CLUBS FOR THE NEXT FEW YEARS, HE CAN BUY ONE WHEN HE RETIRES.
— *Gerard Houllier*
on Steven Gerrard

IF WE AIM FOR THE MOON, MAYBE WE'LL LAND AMONG THE STARS.
— *Gerard Houllier on the*
successful quest for the 2001
Treble

THE BEST STRIKERS HAVE TO BE SELFISH.
— *Ian Rush*

REPUTATIONS DO NOT MEAN ANYTHING TO ME. IF THEY DID, I WOULD CHOOSE IAN RUSH AND ROGER HUNT UP FRONT.
— *Gerard Houllier*

STEVEN GERRARD IS SOUNESS WITH PACE AND THAT'S A HELL OF A PLAYER.
— *Alan Hansen*

SUPER QUIZ

P

U

Z

Z

L

E

1. From which club did Liverpool sign Milan Baros?

2. Who is the only Liverpool player to score a hat-trick on his League debut for the Reds?

3. True or false – Stephane Henchoz hasn't scored for Liverpool.

4. Which former player has appeared against Liverpool in a European Cup Final and FA Cup Final, for different clubs?

5. When Liverpool beat Everton 3–2 in the derby at Goodison Park in 1985, which Reds striker scored after just 20 seconds?

6. At which ground did Gerard Houllier win his first game as sole Liverpool manager?

7. Name the odd man out – Emlyn Hughes, Phil Thompson, Phil Neal and Graeme Souness?

8. Who were Liverpool's first-ever opponents in the Premier League?

9. Name the former West Brom full-back who would have joined Liverpool in the mid-eighties but for failing a medical?

10. Why was Terry McDermott's goal in the 1978 League Cup Final replay disallowed – handball, foul or offside?

11. Liverpool have competed in the World Club Championship twice – who were their opponents?

12. In which year did Anfield become an all-seater stadium?

13. Which comprehensive school in Liverpool did Steven Gerrard attend?

14. Who was the last Liverpool player to represent Northern Ireland in a full international?

15. What happened next? – Wembley Stadium, 1988, Peter Beardsley shrugs off an illegal challenge by Andy Thorn and cleverly chips the ball over Wimbledon goalkeeper Dave Beasant and into the net...

P

A

G

E

S

WHO am I?

Who am I? – I was born in Barrow-in-Furness, in 1947. My first club was Blackpool and I joined Liverpool in 1967. As captain of the Reds I lifted the League title, FA Cup, UEFA Cup and European Cup. My nickname was 'Crazy Horse'.

My name is...

I was born in Chester. I scored my first Liverpool goal against Wimbledon and my first England goal against Chile. I was England's top scorer in the 2002 World Cup and I am celebrating the birth of my first daughter this year.

My name is...

ODD ONE OUT

Name the odd ones out from the following lists and explain why:

1. Michael Owen, Danny Murphy, Steven Gerrard, Sami Hyypia

2. Graeme Souness, Kevin Keegan, Ian Rush, Kenny Dalglish

3. Bruce Grobbelaar, David James, Mike Hooper, Sander Westerveld

4. Paris, Rome, London, Madrid

5. Man Utd, Spurs, Bolton, Everton

I signed for Liverpool from Lille in June 2002, and am a full French international. I made my Anfield debut in a pre-season friendly against Lazio, where I won the Man of the Match award. I scored my first Liverpool goal against Spartak Moscow in last season's Champions League.

My name is...

I have previously played for Blackburn Rovers in the Premiership. I am a full international with my country but I am yet to score my first goal for Liverpool. I missed the second half of last season because I needed a calf operation.

My name is...

I missed the last World Cup because of injury. The Liverpool manager nicknamed me 'Platini' during the season. I was voted the club's Player of the Season for last year on Liverpool's official website.

My name is...

All answers on page 63

HYYPIA AND
—ANFIELD'S SOLID

HENCHOZ BRICK WALL

LFC'S TOP DEFENSIVE DUO REVEAL THE SECRETS BEHIND THE PARTNERSHIP THAT PROVIDES THE REDS WITH MUCH-NEEDED STABILITY AT THE BACK

Liverpool's well-publicised defensive problems during the traumatic nineties came to an end as soon as Gerard Houllier paired Finnish skipper Sami Hyypia with Swiss star Stephane Henchoz at the heart of his back line. Where once opposing attackers scored goals for fun, they were now continually running into the brick wall of a sensational new-look Reds defence.

Stephane Henchoz was well-known to the Premiership having arrived at Liverpool from Blackburn Rovers, but Hyypia's arrival from little-known Dutch outfit Willem II raised more than one or two eyebrows in the footballing world.

The sceptics needn't have worried – Hyypia soon made a nonsense of his paltry £2 million transfer fee with a series of performances which will probably lead to him being labelled Gerard Houllier's greatest-ever buy.

The leadership qualities of Hyypia, allied with the no-nonsense style of Henchoz, ensured Liverpool were no longer a soft touch at the back. Goals were no longer needlessly conceded and opponents had to work harder than ever to breach the rock-like defensive line which greeted them within sight of the Reds' goal. But what makes this partnership work? Why is it so water-tight and so difficult to penetrate?

SAMI HYYPIA

I really enjoy playing alongside Stephane because we have built up a good understanding of each other's game over the last few seasons. Often we don't even need to talk to each other to know where the other person is going to be on the field. We know each other's game so well and I think that helps to build up unity and understanding in defence.

Obviously it's important that your two centre-backs gel, otherwise you will have problems. But it's not all about the men in the middle at the back. Everyone in the team, including strikers, has to work hard to defend and close people down.

My partnership with Stephane clicked from the start really. He is a terrific defender who is very difficult to get past. We have great confidence in each other's game and that helps. If you're worrying about what your defensive partner is doing, or about where they are on the field, then you can't concentrate on your own game.

We work hard every day in training to improve all the time and so far everything has been going well. Our defensive record is good and I think we had the best goals-conceded record in the league a year or so ago.

It's hard to explain why we work so well together. It's all about an understanding and appreciation of the play as well as of each other's game. We rarely go out socialising together outside of working hours, but we have a good friendship in training and on the field and maybe we're seeing the results of that.

But, I repeat, if we've had a good record in defence over recent seasons then it's not just because of two players. Everyone deserves some credit for that.

STEPHANE HENCHOZ

Sami has been absolutely brilliant since he first came into the team and I can't speak too highly about how consistent his performances have been for the team.

When I came to Liverpool I knew I'd be able to compete in the Premiership because I spent time at Blackburn, and so in that sense it was never going to be new for me. But foreigners coming to England from another league can take time to settle in and some people will have wondered how long it would take Sami to get used to English football. I don't think it took him any time at all. He took to it like a duck to water and he has been one of our best players since he has been here.

He is the captain of the team and his performances lead by example. I think we have developed a good partnership, but at the same time it's also important from the club's point of view to realise there are other players, like Djimi Traore, who can come in and do a job if either Sami or I pick up an injury.

The standards at Liverpool are incredibly high and I know we're always very disappointed when we concede a goal. Sometimes there is nothing you can do because the opposition score a great goal, but usually there will be things we can look at later and say we could have done something to prevent it. So while we're happy with our defensive understanding, it's important that we keep working hard to maintain our standards.

It's been an amazing year for you, hasn't it?

Yes, it's gone better than I could have hoped for really. I've benefited from training on a daily basis with the first team at Melwood and I think I have improved as the season has gone on. I've scored goals for the reserve team on a regular basis and the manager has included me in some first team squads so I'm happy with that. But I want to keep on improving and keep on staking my claim for more chances in the first team.

How much did you enjoy scoring your first senior goal at Sheffield United?

That was a brilliant moment for me. It was soured a bit because we lost the game in the end – even though we went through in the tie overall. It was a typical goal for me – six yards out and pretty unmissable! To score that goal at the end where all the Liverpool fans were and to hear them singing my name was brilliant. It was definitely one of the highlights of my career so far, but hopefully there are many more to come.

Who was your boyhood hero?

My boyhood idol was Alan Shearer, he was just different class. Everywhere he has been he has been absolutely brilliant. He scores goals and his hold-up play is fantastic. I would like to say I model myself on him but I am nowhere near as good as him. He is someone I would like to model myself on and be a similar player. I grew up a Man City fan and so I would also say that Shaun Goater is a player I really admire. I'm like him in that if I come off the field at the end of a game having not scored a goal then I'm disappointed. I'm on the pitch to score goals and that's what I want to do.

Tell us a bit about your family and your interests outside football?

I've got one older brother who is 28 and a PE teacher, as well as an elder sister who is 26 and an air hostess. She does a lot of long-haul flights and was in Milwaukee when I scored that goal against Sheffield United! I've got a twin sister but she's four minutes younger than me so I'm older. She's at university in Leeds. She feels left out because I'm getting all the attention but she's alright about it. They are very supportive of me. Outside football I enjoy simple things like listening to music, playing other sports and snooker.

TIP FOR THE TOP

SON OF FORMER MANCHESTER CITY FOOTBALLER IAN, NEIL MELLOR HAS AN UNCANNY ABILITY TO SCORE GOALS – 56 IN ALL COMPETITIONS LAST YEAR INCLUDING ONE IN SIX APPEARANCES FOR THE FIRST TEAM. COULD THIS BE THE SEASON HE BREAKS THROUGH?

Who is your best mate in the Liverpool squad?
John Welsh, Stephen Warnock, Jon Otsemobor. We all have a laugh and a bit of banter which is good.

Your dad (former professional Ian Mellor) says you haven't done anything in the game yet, so are you going to be a better player than he was and make him eat his words?
I'd love to make him eat his words! No, he's right I haven't achieved anything yet. If I'm being honest I have achieved getting into Liverpool's first team which for me is a major achievement. But considering what he achieved in his career I would love to do well and make him eat his words!

What can you learn off striker coach Ian Rush?
Anything I can learn off Ian Rush would be a bonus. What a great goalscorer he was and an idol. The fans still sing his name, Rush scores one, Rush scores two, you know they sing it every game. He can teach me different ways of getting in the box and movement which would be helpful.

How has your life changed since you got a chance with the first team – anything noticeable?
Nothing amazing really. My dad's career seems to have started again and he has had a lot of hassle and people talking about me, but for me it has been all right.

There must be some changes?
I suppose I get recognised a bit more now, but not to anything like the level that the likes of Michael Owen and Steven Gerrard get. I just want to concentrate on doing my job as well as I possibly can and to keep improving. I know the manager must rate me otherwise he wouldn't have offered me a new contract last season. I was happy to sign that because I want to stay at this club and I want to keep on improving. I'm working with the best people in the best facilities and I can only benefit from that.

Where do you see yourself in 10 years' time and where would you like to be?
I'd love to be a Liverpool first-team regular and scoring lots and lots of goals and helping us to win loads of trophies. I would also like to play for England in a World Cup.

DOB 28 JANUARY 1978 **NATIONALITY** ENGLISH **POSITION** DEFENDER **NICKNAME** CARRA
HEIGHT 6' 1 **WEIGHT** 12st 10lbs **SQUAD NUMBER** 23 **PREVIOUS CLUBS** NONE

JAMIE CARRAGHER

1. In which year did Jamie help the Reds to win the FA Youth Cup?
2. When did he sign professional forms with Liverpool?
3. Against which team did he make his debut for the club?
4. Against which team did he score his first goal for the club?
5. What record does he hold at England Under-21 level?
6. When did he win his first full England cap?
7. Against which country did he do that?
8. In which position did he play most games during the Treble season?
9. Which injury ruled him out of the England squad for the 2002 World Cup?
10. Against who did he wear the England captain's armband for the first time?

All answers on page 63

+ + + SAMMY LEE COMBINES HIS ROLE AS LIVERPOOL COACH WITH A JOB ON ENGLAND'S COACHING TEAM + + JOHN

> **1** In which year did Danny sign for Liverpool?
>
> **2** How much did he cost?
>
> **3** Which club did he join on loan during the 1998–1999 season?
>
> **4** Which of Liverpool's three major cup finals in 2001 did he miss out on?
>
> **5** Against which country did he make his international debut?
>
> **6** Which French footballing legend has Houllier compared him to?
>
> **7** Did Danny go to the World Cup in 2002?
>
> **8** Where did he score his only England goal in the 4–0 defeat of Paraguay on April 17 2002?
>
> **9** Who replaced him in the 2002 World Cup squad after his injury?
>
> **10** How many cup finals has he scored in for Liverpool?

DOB 18 MARCH 1977 **NATIONALITY** ENGLISH **POSITION** MIDFIELDER **NICKNAME** SPUD
HEIGHT 5'9 **WEIGHT** 12st 8lbs **SQUAD NUMBER** 13 **PREVIOUS CLUBS** CREWE ALEXANDRA

DANNY MURPHY

THE ROOF WAS PUT ON THE SPION KOP IN 1928 + + + + + + +LIVERPOOL'S ANTHEM

'Walk on...'

WHEN GERRY MARSDEN BELLOWED OUT HIS WORLD FAMOUS ANTHEM BEFORE LIVERPOOL'S UEFA CUP CLASH AT CELTIC BACK IN MARCH, NOT ONE SUPPORTER INSIDE PARKHEAD THAT NIGHT WOULD HAVE HAD A DRY EYE

Scarves were held aloft and voices raised as everyone – whether they were wearing red or green and white – sang along to a song that means to much to both clubs.

'You'll Never Walk Alone' isn't just a footballing song. It's THE footballing anthem. Adopted by Liverpool fans back in the sixties when Gerry and his Pacemakers enjoyed a number one hit with it, YNWA has been passed on from generation to generation and is still sung as enthusiastically and as passionately by Reds fans today.

There's no doubt that it was the Kopites who first aired the song at a football ground – but no one would deny the Celtic fans their right to adopt it as their tune as well.

There are few better atmospheres in world football than when Celtic meet Liverpool. Whether it be a testimonial game or a match of high importance in European competition, the fans always rise to the occasion and turn it into an event to savour.

It was no different last March when, with just minutes to go before the first leg of a crucial UEFA Cup quarter final kicked off, Gerry Marsden united both sets of fans as one with a stirring rendition of his great anthem.

"That was one of the greatest occasions of my entire life," he said later. "I was excited at the prospect of doing it, but the reality was even better.

"To hear the two best sets of supporters in the world singing a song that means so much to me is just fantastic.

"Bill Shankly once said to me ,'Son, I have given Liverpool a team, but you have given them a song. On that night it felt like it was everyone's song – and that made it extra special.

"There was only a small corner of the ground that was red and white, but you could hear them as loud as ever with the Celtic fans."

As far as the match was concerned, Celtic made a dream start and opened the scoring after just two minutes when Henrik Larsson knocked home Alan Thompson's left wing cross from close range, but Liverpool levelled before the break when Emile Heskey took John Arne Riise's pass in his stride and fired a first time shot low into the far corner.

Celtic eventually triumphed in the tie following a 2–0 win at Anfield a week later when, once again, both sets of fans did Gerry Marsden proud by singing his anthem while holding their scarves and flags aloft.

It's a legendary story of two football clubs and one song – let's hope it's a story which has many more chapters to it over the coming years. ⊕

LIVERPOOL CELTIC

STÉPHANE HENCHOZ

DOB 7 SEPTEMBER 1974 **NATIONALITY** SWISS **POSITION** DEFENDER **NICKNAME** STEPH
HEIGHT 6' 2 **WEIGHT** 12st 8lbs **SQUAD NUMBER** 2 **PREVIOUS CLUBS** STADE PAYERNE, BULLE, XAMAX NEUCHATEL, SV HAMBURG, BLACKBURN ROVERS

> 1 Where in Switzerland was Stephane born?
> 2 Which English-born coach signed him for Neuchetal Xamas?
> 3 Which accolade did he win with Blackburn in the 1998–99 season?
> 4 How much did Gerard Houllier pay to bring him to Anfield?
> 5 Why was his Liverpool debut delayed after he signed for the club?
> 6 Against which team and in which competition did he make his Reds debut?
> 7 How many World Cups has he played in for his country?
> 8 How many goals has he scored for Liverpool?
> 9 What operation did he require in March 2003?
> 10 He made a decision during 2002 which he reversed in 2003. What was it?

All answers on page 63

> 1 Which trophy did Sami win with MyPa in 1992?
> 2 Against which country did he make his international debut?
> 3 In what year did he move to Holland to play for Willem?
> 4 What did he help Liverpool's defence achieve during the 1999–2000 season?
> 5 How many red or yellow cards did he pick up during season 2000–2001?
> 6 When was he appointed Liverpool captain?
> 7 Which award did he win in Finland during 2002?
> 8 Has he scored more than 10 goals for Liverpool?
> 9 "Her-pee-a", "Hoo-pee-a" or "Hi-pee-a": which is the correct pronounciation of his surname?
> 10 Who did he first lift the FA Cup aloft with after the 2001 FA Cup final?

DOB 7 OCTOBER 1973 **NATIONALITY** FINNISH **POSITION** DEFENDER **NICKNAME** SAMI
HEIGHT 6' 3 **WEIGHT** 13st 5lbs **SQUAD NUMBER** 4 **PREVIOUS CLUBS** PALLO-PEIKOT, KUMU, MYPA ANJALANKOSKI, WILLEM II

SAMI HYYPIA

FIXTURES >>>>

BARCLAYCARD PREMIERSHIP

DATE	OPPOSITION	RESULT	SCORERS	STAR MAN
August 17	CHELSEA (H)			
August 23	Aston Villa (A)			
August 27	TOTTENHAM (H)			
August 30	Everton (A)			
September 13	Blackburn (A)			
September 20	LEICESTER (H)			
September 27	Charlton (A)			
October 4	ARSENAL (H)			
October 18	Portsmouth (A)			
October 25	LEEDS (H)			
November 1	Fulham (A)			
November 9	MANCHESTER UNITED (H)			
November 22	Middlesbrough (A)			
November 29	BIRMINGHAM (H)			
December 6	Newcastle (A)			
December 13	SOUTHAMPTON (H)			
December 20	Wolverhampton (A)			
December 26	BOLTON (H)			
December 28	Manchester City (A)			
January 7 2004	Chelsea (A)			
January 10	ASTON VILLA (H)			
January 17	Tottenham (A)			
January 31	EVERTON (H)			
February 7	Bolton (A)			
February 11	MANCHESTER CITY (H)			
February 21	PORTSMOUTH (H)			
February 28	Leeds (A)			
March 13	Southampton (A)			
March 20	WOLVERHAMPTON (H)			
March 27	Leicester (A)			
April 3	BLACKBURN (H)			
April 10	Arsenal (A)			
April 12	CHARLTON (H)			
April 17	FULHAM (H)			
April 24	Manchester United (A)			
May 1	MIDDLESBROUGH (H)			
May 8	Birmingham (A)			
May 15	NEWCASTLE (H)			

All fixtures are correct at time of going to press, but are subject to change

+ + + + + JACK BALMER ONCE SCORED HAT-TRICKS IN THREE SUCCESSIVE MATCHES FOR LIVERPOOL + + + + +